Ibiza Island of Dreams
2nd Edition

Ibiza Island of Dreams - 2nd Edition focuses on the paradise Spanish holiday island of Ibiza in the warm Mediterranean blue azure sea explored in words and pictures. Susie and I have holidayed on the island several times in the past and found, for us, it was a journey to the Island of our Dreams.

by Norfolk Watercolour Artist - Alan R. Massen
Published in Great Britain by Rainbow Publications UK

First Published in 2016 by Rainbow Publications UK
2nd Edition Published in 2019 by Rainbow Publications UK

Copyright © 2019 Alan R. Massen

The moral right of Alan R. Massen to be identified as the author of this work has been asserted in accordance with the UK Copyright, Designs and Patents Act of 1988. All rights reserved.

No part of this book may be reproduced, or stored in a retrieval system, or transmitted in any form or by any means, electronic, mechanical, photocopying, recording, or otherwise, without the prior written permission of both the author and the above publisher of this book All imagery and illustrations

© Alan R. Massen

Neither the publisher nor the author can accept liability for the use of any of the materials, methods or information recommended in this book or for any consequences arising out of their use, nor can they be held responsible for any errors or omissions that may be found in the text or may occur at a future date as a result of changes in rules, laws or equipment All manufacturers, sellers, product names and services identified in this book are used in editorial fashion and for the benefit of such companies with no intention of any infringement of trademarks. No such use or the use of any trade name is intended to convey endorsement or other affiliation with this book

Paperback Edition ISBN 978-0-9933962-6-7
Typeset in Minion Pro
Published in Great Britain by Rainbow Publications UK

About the Author

Alan was born in the city of Norwich in the county of Norfolk, England in November 1949. When Alan was still a teenager he started painting whilst attending art classes in Norwich. In his mid-teens he had two paintings accepted for a National Art Exhibition held in London and other major UK cities. Alan spent most of his working life as a professional Health and Safety Advisor and rarely picked up a paint brush until he, his wife Susie and daughter Ginny (his other daughter Mandy is married and lives with her husband Adrian in Sheffield) moved out of the city of Norwich into the countryside in 1993. They moved to a little village called East Lexham in the heart of Norfolk. The village was very peaceful and pretty. This helped inspire Alan to take up watercolour painting once again. In 2004 they moved to another small West Norfolk village near Downham Market where they still live today. In 2008 Alan had to retire due to ill health (bad knees) and whilst he still painted regularly he began to spend more and more time gardening. In 2013 his wife Susie suggested that he kept a gardening diary to record his adventures in the garden and capture the changing seasons, animals, birds and the successes and failures of being a gardener he encountered. By the following year Susie suggested that he should write a book from his diary and include illustrations of both the garden and his artwork. In 2014 Alan's first book was published by Creative Gateway called **"Retiring to the Garden – Year One"**. This proved such a success that Alan decided to follow this up with his second book called **"Retiring into a Rainbow"** featuring his watercolour paintings. He then in 2015 published **"Retiring to Our Garden – Year Two"** published this time by Rainbow Publications UK. He then re-issued his first two books this time in a **"Second Edition"**. Also published by Rainbow Publications UK. In 2016-2019 he published: **"Skiathos a Greek Island Paradise"**, **"Norfolk the County of my Birth"**, **"Art Inspired by a Rainbow"** and **"Ibiza Island of Dreams"**. He has recently completed three new books which are entitled **"Flip-flops and Shades on Thassos"**, **"Majorca Island in the Sun"** and finally **"Mardle and a Troshin' in Norfolk"** and these will be published by Rainbow Publications UK in the near future.

I hope you enjoy my Ibiza book…

Book by the same Author
Retiring to the Garden – Year 1

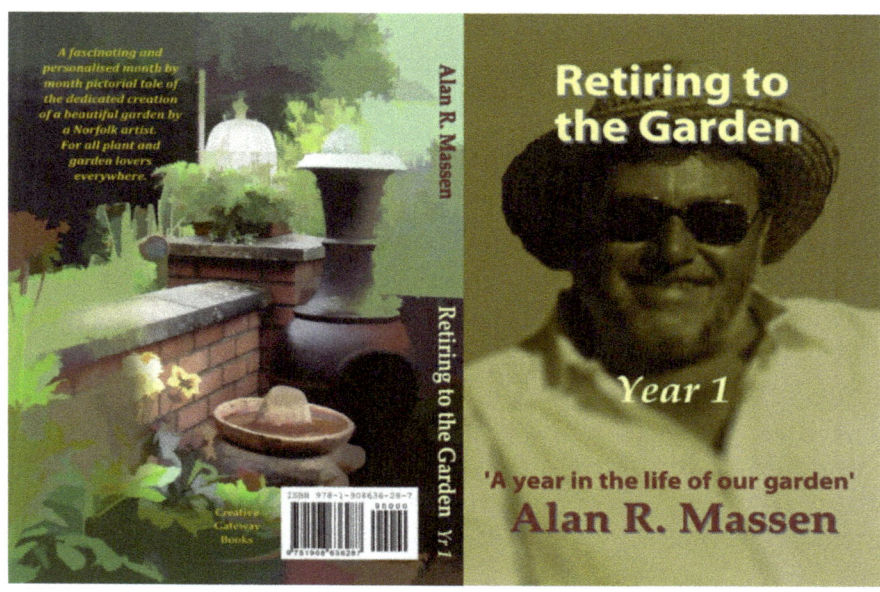

A fascinating and personalised month by month pictorial tale of the dedicated creation of a beautiful garden by Norfolk watercolour artist Alan R. Massen.

by Norfolk Watercolour Artist - Alan R. Massen
Published in Great Britain by Creative Gateway

Book by the same Author
Retiring into a Rainbow - 2nd Edition

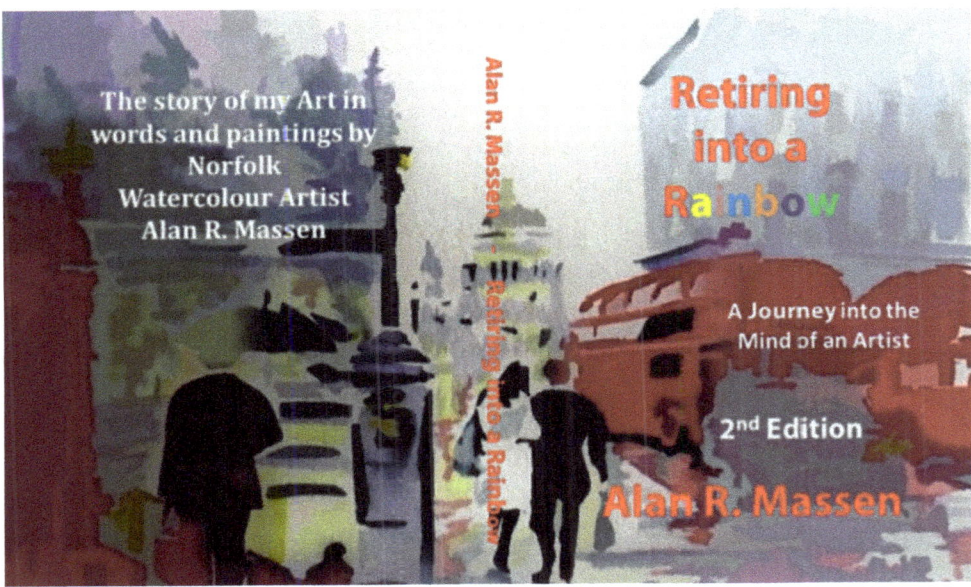

This beautifully illustrated book will take you through an incredible journey into the mind of Norfolk watercolour artist Alan R. Massen as he describes the inspiration, background and emotional meaning behind a large selection of his paintings, created over a period of more than twenty years…

by Norfolk Watercolour Artist - Alan R. Massen
Published 1st Edition by Creative Gateway and 2nd Edition by Rainbow Publications UK

Book by the same Author
Retiring to Our Garden – Year Two

The continuation of the fascinating and personalised month by month pictorial tale of the dedicated creation of a beautiful garden which is now in its second year by Norfolk artist Alan R. Massen.

by Norfolk Watercolour Artist - Alan R. Massen
Published in Great Britain by Rainbow Publications UK

Book by the same Author
Retiring to Our Garden – Year One

A fascinating and personalised month by month pictorial tale of the dedicated creation of a beautiful garden by Norfolk Watercolour Artist Alan R. Massen.

by Norfolk Watercolour Artist - Alan R. Massen
Published 1st Edition by Creative Gateway and 2nd Edition by Rainbow Publications UK

Book by the same Author
Skiathos a Greek Island Paradise

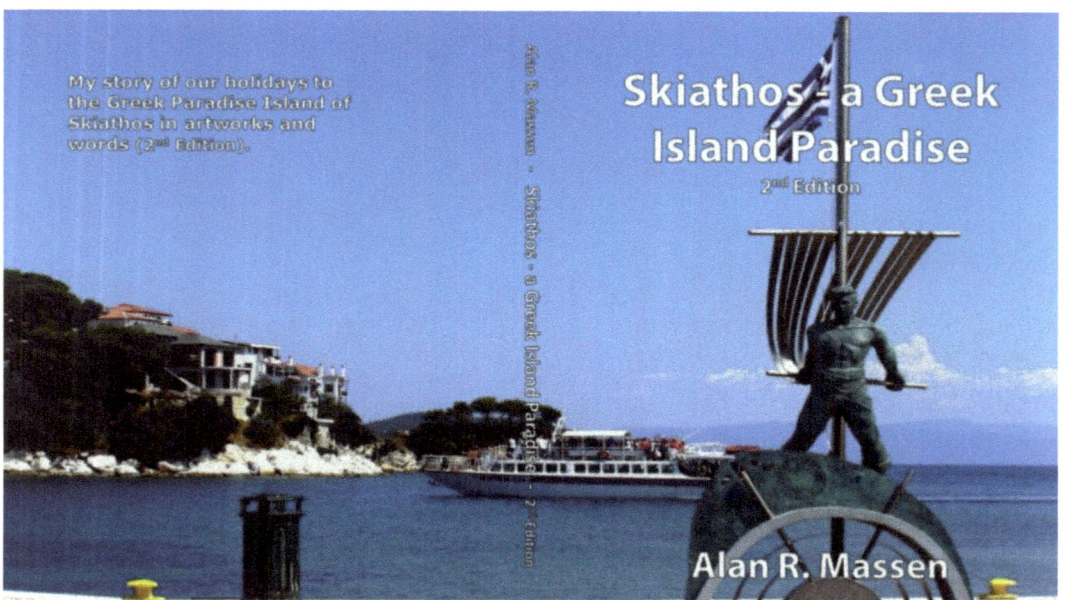

This beautifully illustrated book will take you through an incredible journey to the beautiful Greek Island of Skiathos which is the best known of the Sporades Islands. People are drawn by the allure of its beaches along with pretty villages, pine covered hills and a perfect climate.

by Norfolk Watercolour Artist - Alan R. Massen
Published in Great Britain by Rainbow Publications UK

Book by the same Author

Norfolk the County of my Birth

A celebration of the County of the authors birth in which Norfolk Watercolour Artist Alan R. Massen takes the reader on an artwork journey around Norfolk.

by Norfolk Watercolour Artist - Alan R. Massen
Published in Great Britain by Rainbow Publications UK

Book by the same Author

Art Inspired by a Rainbow

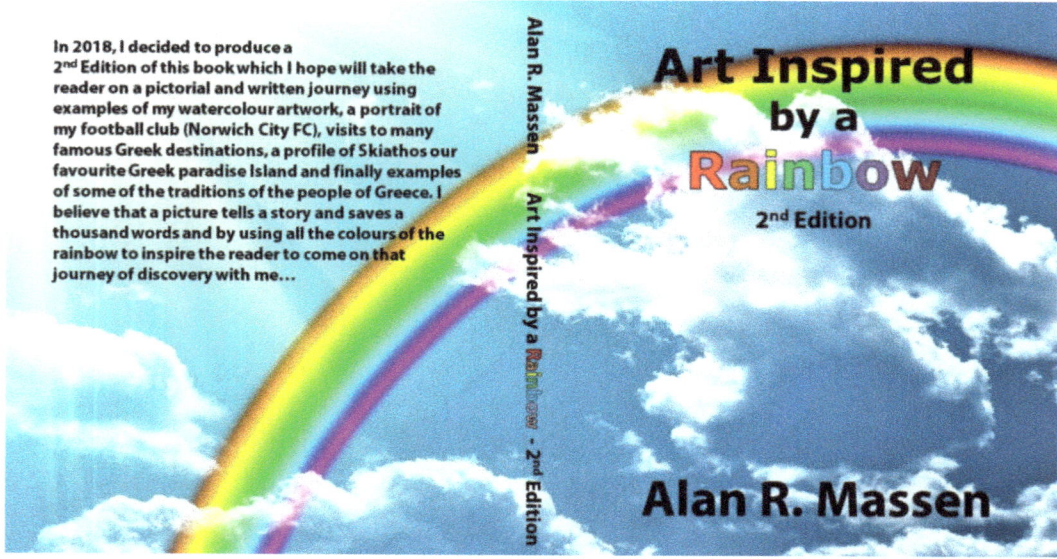

In 2018, Alan R. Massen, the Norfolk watercolour artist, decided to produce this book which he hopes will take the reader on a pictorial journey using some of his favourite paintings and artworks.

By Norfolk Watercolour Artist Alan R. Massen
Published in Great Britain by Rainbow Publications UK

Book by the same Author

Ibiza Island of Dreams

Ibiza Island of Dreams focuses on the paradise Spanish holiday island of Ibiza in the warm Mediterranean blue azure sea explored in words and pictures.

by Norfolk Watercolour Artist - Alan R. Massen
Published in Great Britain by Rainbow Publications UK

Book by the same Author

Flip-flops and Shades on Thassos

The paradise Greek holiday island of Thassos in the warm Mediterranean blue azure sea explored in words and pictures.

by Norfolk Watercolour Artist Alan R. Massen
Published in Great Britain by Rainbow Publications UK

Book by the same Author

Majorca Island in the Sun

Majorca Island in the Sun focuses on the paradise Spanish holiday island of Majorca in the warm Mediterranean blue azure sea explored in words and pictures. We have holidayed on the island in the past and it really is a journey into the sunshine.

by Norfolk Watercolour Artist Alan R. Massen
Published in Great Britain by Rainbow Publications UK

Book by the same Author

Mardle and a Troshin' in Norfolk

A Journey through ten months in my life in Norfolk in 2015 - 2016 explored in words and artwork pictures. "An old Norfolk boys ramblings".

by Norfolk Watercolour Artist Alan R. Massen
Published in Great Britain by Rainbow Publications UK

Dedication

Welcome to my book that features the Spanish paradise Island of Ibiza. I would like to dedicate this publication to our good friends Alistair, Issy, Karl, Anna, Andrew and Lynn who like us love their holidays in the Mediterranean.

Susie and Alan in Portinax on Ibiza

Susie on Portinatx beach on Ibiza…

I hope you will enjoy visiting Ibiza with us…

Contents

Introduction to Ibiza…………………….	1
Ibiza History, Climate and Geography…	5
Facts About Ibiza ……………………..	11
Out and About on Ibiza ………………….	18
Exploring Ibiza ….……………………	26
Ibiza Town ………….…..…………….	129
Ibiza in Colour ….…….…..…………….	145
Acknowledgement …………………..	202

Copyright © 2019 Alan R. Massen

Introduction to Ibiza

Situated just of the coast of Valencia, Ibiza is in the Spanish Balearic Islands group and is known across the world as being the party capital of the world. But forget the stereotypical British abroad images you may have of Ibiza, this only accounts for a small part of the island. Step away from the noisy streets of San Antonio's infamous strip and you will find a magical island, which can cater for your every need. We have had several of our summer holidays on Ibiza over the years and have always enjoyed ourselves. Susie and I have stayed in both the busy San Antonio Bay and the more relaxed resort of Portinatx. We have toured the island by hire car and also on the local buses. Head to the northern part of the island and you'll find a peaceful and tranquil destination, popular with families. On the south-east side of the island you will find the beautiful and historic Ibiza Town, as well as the hugely popular Playa D'en Bossa. Head West and you'll hit San Antonio and if you want to stay this side of the island, there are some great hotels and fantastic haunts that will make sure your holiday is all that you hoped and wanted it to be...

Introduction to Ibiza:

Although Ibiza is renowned for having some of the best nightclubs in the world, the island also has an absolutely beautiful coastline with dozens of tiny coves to discover, not to mention some of the most stylish hotels in the Mediterranean. We have stayed in both apartments and hotels on the island but we have always stayed on a bed and breakfast basis. This was so we could either have other meals where we were staying or more often than not venture out of the accommodation to sample the local dishes in restaurant's and/or beach side cafes nearby…

Introduction to Ibiza:

If you choose to explore Ibiza in the autumn and winter, you will get a much better idea of the real Ibiza, particularly if you also delve into the island's rich history. Although the tourist season really gets going in May and winds down again in October, the island is really very beautiful in early spring when the almond blossom are out. Outside the hottest months of July and August, all the Balearics are good for activity holidays, whether you want to enjoy the easy type or the more challenging…

Introduction to Ibiza:

On Ibiza there is plenty to see if you are interested in plants or wildlife. Sunshine is not always guaranteed, however, and you may well hit a rainy patch in late autumn. In peak season you can stay for a week of wild partying, staying in the lively resorts of Playa d'en Bossa or San Antonio. Susie and I have stayed in and visited both of these resorts and we enjoyed our stay very much. On the other hand, Santa Eulalia is more laid back with plenty of waterfront bars, restaurants and gift shops which Susie and I have spent many a happy hour wandering around. For a cultural fix, explore the hilltop Dalt Vila fortress in Ibiza Town, then come back down and slide into a pavement café for a refreshing cold drink. Both the islands coast and countryside are beautiful in spring and autumn, when you can enjoy a relaxing walking or cycling holiday. Now that we have comes to an end of my introduction, we will, in the next chapter read about the History, Climate and Geography of Ibiza…

The History, Climate and Geography of Ibiza

Like all island in the Mediterranean Ibiza has had a long and interesting past and it is well worthwhile reviewing some of their history. In 654 BC, the Phoenician settlers founded a port on the Balearic Island of Ibiza this was called Ibossim from the Phoenician Iboshim meaning dedicated to the Egyptian god of music and dance Bes. If like me you are fascinated by the Egypt of ancient times it is great to know that even in those times the Phoenician associated music and dance with Ibiza. It is nice to know that the island reputation for loud and vibrant music and dance lives on today. When the Romans came to Ibiza they called it Ebusus and mined and exported goods and valuables back to Rome from the islands port. The Greeks called the island of Ibiza and the nearby island of Formentera by the name of Pityussai. This is the Greek word for pine covered islands…

Ibiza History:

Ibiza Town harbour today is filled with luxury yachts and not the cargo boats that would have used the port years ago. Back to the past and after the decline of the Phoenicians there was an invasion by the Assyrians. This meant that Ibiza came under the control of Carthage which was also a former Phoenician colony. At this time Ibiza was a major trading post along the Mediterranean routes producing dye, salt, fish sauce (garum) and wool. Ibiza established its own trading stations on the nearby Balearic island of Majorca. Taking this action meant that Ibiza was beginning to become an important provider of goods to many places both near and far…

Ibiza History:

The Island negotiated a favourable treaty with the Romans, which spared Ibiza from further destruction and allowed it to continue its Carthaginian-Punic institutions well into the Empire days, when it became an official Roman municipality. For this reason, Ibiza today contains excellent examples of late Carthaginian-Punic civilisation. During the Roman Empire, the island became a quiet imperial outpost, removed from the important trading routes of the time. After the fall of the Western Roman Empire and for a brief period of first Vandal and the Byzantine rule, the island was conquered by the Moors in 990 AD and the locals converted to Islam and Berber settlers came to the island…

Ibiza History:

In more recent times Ibiza together with the islands of Formentera and Minorca were invaded by the Norwegian King Sigurd I of Norway in the spring of 1110 AD whilst he was on his way to the crusade in Jerusalem. This was not however, the end of foreign invasions of Ibiza as it was then conquered by King James I in 1235 AD. The local Muslim population got deported as was the case with neighbouring Majorca and other small islands elsewhere, and Christians then arrived from Girona. The island of Ibiza maintained its own self-government in several forms right up until 1715 AD, when King Philip V of Spain abolished the local government's autonomy. Coming right up to date the arrival of democracy in the late 1970's led to the Statute of Autonomy of the Balearic Islands. Today, the island is part of the Balearic Autonomous Community which consists of Ibiza, Majorca, Minorca and Formentera. The official name of the island in Catalan is "Eivissa"…

The Climate of Ibiza:

The sunshine index for the Island of Ibiza:

January 5+ hours
February 7 hours
March 7+ hours
April 8 hours
May 12 hours
June 12+ hours
July 14+ hours
August 14+ hours
September 11+ hours
October 10 hours
November 7 hours
December 6 hours

The Temperature for the Island of Ibiza:

The summer climate of Ibiza typically ranges in the upper 20 °C (70-80 °F), often reaching 30.0 °C (86 °F), with overnight lows below 22.2 °C (72 °F).

The winter, off-season temperature reaches lows of 8.1–14.2 °C (46.6–57.6 °F), with highs in the upper-teens °C (60 °F).

So the island of Ibiza is an ideal place to go for those who want the sun or to see the wonderful countryside, wildlife and flowers dependant on when you go…

The Geography of Ibiza:

Alan in Portinatx…

Above we see Alan enjoying the view of the resort from his seat on a wall in Portinatx where we stayed in apartments for two of our summer holidays on the island and enjoyed our stay there very much. Ibiza is a rocky island covering an area of 572.56 square kilometres (221.07 square miles), almost six times smaller than Majorca. Ibiza however, is the largest of a group of the Western Balearic archipelago called the "Pityuses" or "Pine Islands" composed of itself and the island of Formentera. The Balearic island chain includes over 50 islands, many of which are uninhabited. The highest point of the island is Sa Talaissa, at 475 metres (1,558 feet). At the 2001 census Ibiza had a total population of 88,076 inhabitants, which had risen to an estimated 132,637 by the start of 2010. These figures are substantially increased in the summer months by tourists. Having read about the History, Climate and Geography of Ibiza it is now time, in the next chapter to read about some facts about Ibiza…

Facts about Ibiza

The People of Ibiza:

All the local Spanish people that we met during our stays on the island of Ibiza have been very friendly and helpful just like the local man on the glass bottom boat with Susie and Ginny above. They take great pride in their island and everywhere we went was kept clean and tidy and the beaches were brushed and cleaned every day. Unlike the UK, the local bus drivers were very helpful and were happy to give advice on bus times and pickup points. Wherever we went to eat the staff were friendly and although the food was sometimes too touristy for our tastes everywhere was clean and the food was hot and flavoursome. The people of Ibiza share their island not just with tourists but they also have a large number of foreign migrant workers that have been incorporated over the years, into the culture of the island very successfully. Nothing is too much trouble for the local people that we came into contact with and they always answered any request we had with a "no problem"…

Facts - The People of Ibiza:

The islands population in terms of origin, about 55 percent of island residents were born on Ibiza, 35 percent are domestic migrants from mainland Spain (mostly working-class families from Andalusia, and the rest are from Catalonia, Valencia and Castile), and the remaining 10 to 15 percent are foreign, dual and multi-national citizens of the EU and abroad. In decreasing order, the foreigners on the island today are Germans, British, Latin Americans, French, Italians, Dutch, in addition to a myriad of other nationalities…

Facts - Famous People of Ibiza:

Above we see Susie looking out over Ibiza Town from the Old Town and Alan once more is all at sea. Ibiza has several famous sons among's these are the Spanish composer and music theorist Miguel Roig-Francoli who was born on Ibiza, as was the politician and Spain's former Minister of Foreign Affairs, Abel Matutes. Ibiza is also a popular island for foreigners to make their home and some of the most notable former residents of Ibiza include: English punk musician John Simon Ritchie (Sid Vicious), comic actor Terry Thomas and and film director and actor Orson Wells to name but a few. Much as Susie and I would love to join them I am afraid that we do not have the means to be able to live permanently on the island but we can still nevertheless enjoy a two week stay on the island whenever we can…

Facts - The Language of Ibiza:

On Ibiza the sunsets are very spectacular indeed. Susie and I would always find the time to sit and watch the sun go down wherever we were on Ibiza. On Ibiza Eivissenc is the native dialect of Catalan that is spoken on the island of Ibiza and nearby island of Formentera. The language of Catalan shares co-official status with Spanish. Additionally, because of the influence of tourism and expatriates living in or maintaining residences on the island, other languages like German, English and Italian, are widely spoken. We found that almost all of the locals spoke and understood English and all information in restaurants, cafes, bars and many other places was written in not just Spanish but English as well as in many other languages…

Facts - Tourism on Ibiza:

Above we see Susie enjoying the sunshine by the pool at our apartments in Portinatx on Ibiza. Ibiza is a popular tourist destination, especially due to its legendary and at times riotous nightlife centred on two areas: Ibiza Town, the island's capital on the southern shore and Sant Antonia to the West. In recent years the island's government has been trying to encourage a more cultured and quieter tourism scene, passing rules including the closing of all nightclubs by 6 a.m. at the latest, and requiring all new hotels to be 5-star. The islands administration wants to attract a more international mixture of tourists. Though primarily known for its party scene, large portions of the island are registered as UNESCO World Heritage Sites, and thus protected from the development and commercialisation of the main towns. Notable examples include "God's Finger" in the Benirras Bay as well as some of the more traditional cultural sites such as the remains of the first Phoenicians settlement at Sa Caleta…

Facts - Frequent visitors to Ibiza:

Because of Ibiza's rustic beauty, companies and artists alike frequently use the island for photographic and film shoots. A monument (The Egg) erected in honour of Christopher Columbus can be found in Sant Antonia; Ibiza is one of several places purporting to be his birthplace. Since the early days of mass tourism on the island, there have been a large number of development projects ranging from successful ventures to failed development projects. In 2013, Ibiza property prices generally remained above market value, and many of the development projects on the island have now been completed, as well as some new projects that were announced at the end of 2012. Since 2009, Ibiza has seen an increase in tourist numbers every year, with nearly 6 million people travelling through Ibiza Airport in 2012. The summer season has become concentrated between June and September. The luxury market has dramatically improved, with new restaurants, clubs, and the improvements to the marina in Ibiza Town…

Facts - Cuisine on Ibiza:

Ibiza's local cuisine is typically Mediterranean. One of the most common culinary products of the island is sweets called "flaons" whilst savoury dishes include fish stew and rice with pork. Now that we know some of the facts relating to Ibiza it is now time for us, in the next chapter, to go Out and About on Ibiza …

Out and About on Ibiza

Transport to and within Ibiza:

When we have gone to Ibiza on holiday we have flown from our local airport which is in the city of Norwich in Norfolk. This is only forty minutes from our home so it is a very good choice of holiday destination for us. Ibiza is served by Ibiza airport, which has many international flights during the summer tourist season, especially from the European Union. There are also ferries from the harbour of Sant Antonia and Ibiza Town these go to Barcelona, Majorca, Denia and Valencia. There are also ferries to Formentera leaving Sant Antonia Harbour (normally every Wednesday), and daily from Ibiza Town, Santa Eulària, and Figueretes–Playa d'en Bossa. We have often used the local bus services to get around the island and have found these very useful and reliable…

Out and about on Ibiza: Transport within Ibiza

One of the services we have used whilst on holiday has been the public busses that travel between Sant Antonio and Ibiza Town. These run every 15 minutes in summer and every half hour in winter. In addition, there are buses from Sant Antonia to Cala Bossa, Cala Conta and Cala Tarida, and to the Airport. Susie and I have also used the public buses when travelling to and from Portinatx to Ibiza Town and back and these also were very reliable. From Ibiza Town there are buses also to the Playa d'en Bossa, Ses Salines, the Airport, and Santa Eulària…

Out and about on Ibiza: The Countryside of Ibiza

As a visitor to Ibiza, it is likely that your trip will be mainly centred in the bustling towns and the electrifying nightlife, interspersed with the odd jaunt to one of the many enchanting beaches. Those of you who appreciate the quieter side of Ibiza will know that this magical island has a lot more to offer outside of the bars, clubs and beach. Susie and I have, in the past, walked into the mountainous interior of Ibiza numerous times and found it to be full of wonderful scenery, flowers and wildlife. It is also a great place for crazy golfers like Susie and Ginny!…

Out and about on Ibiza: The Countryside of Ibiza

If you venture just minutes out of town or your resort you are greeted by lush green landscapes, steep rugged hillsides and dusty off-road tracks. Huge orange and lemon orchards, local vineyards and row upon row of olive groves, as far as the eye can see, are the norm, where farmers tending to their herds and crops having never stepped foot into a super club. Instead, their families and friends have been for generations exporting their wares and providing the local eateries and bodegas with organic home grown produce for centuries. Susie and I have often ventured into the hills and villages of Ibiza when on holiday and have enjoyed the views and sampled the local produce sold by the roadside or in the small eating places scattered in the hills and villages…

Out and about on Ibiza: The Countryside of Ibiza

When you are on the island any Ibiza local will tell you that you must explore and discover what they know as 'the campo' or countryside. Take a drive up to the north of the island and find a tiny roadside bar or take a hike on one of the many well documented walking trails and see what it is that makes Ibiza so very special. So, like us, you can: Hire a car, bike or a scooter and head towards the hills and the interior of the island. You are bound to have a fantastic adventure on the way, whilst absorbing the breath taking scenery that envelops this stunning little paradise island…

Out and about on Ibiza: The Night Life and Beyond

When most people think of Ibiza they think of young people, parties and loud music but this is only part of the story as it is also an ideal place to go on a family holiday. Susie and I have taken our daughter Ginny on family holidays there and we have also gone as a couple and enjoyed our stay on the island very much. The beautiful beaches, sea and with plenty to see and do all makes this an ideal choice for all ages. Ibiza might be well known for being a bit of a party island, but there is much more to this Balearic Island than that. Away from the nightlife that is generally focused in resorts such as San Antonio and Playa d'en Bossa, it moves at a far more relaxed and restful pace…

Out and about on Ibiza: The Main Resorts

The Islands Northern Towns like Puerto San Miguel and Portinatx feature sandy coves and beaches, great sea views and hills covered with wild flowers. In recent visits we have stayed in apartments at Portinatx which was ideal for couples and family holidays on the beach with a good selection of shops and restaurants. The beach is ideal and the bay has safe access into the sea. On the South coast of the Island Cala Llonga has a similarly relaxed atmosphere and boasts one of the biggest beaches on the Island. We went there from our resort by tourist train (see above) and it was a great day out. Santa Eulalia, meanwhile, provides a happy medium between lively and laid back. It has boutiques, bars, shops that give it a cosmopolitan feel. The Town has a sweeping pale sandy beach that makes it a favourite with families…

Out and about on Ibiza: Ibiza Town

Ibiza's capital, Ibiza Town, has an old quarter that is cocooned by a Medieval Stone walls and overlooked by a fortress. Susie and Ginny ventured up into the old quarter while I sat at a harbour side bar and had a coffee. The newer part of Town cascades down to the waterfront and has a profusion of shops, bars, restaurants and market stalls. The marina and ferry port are very attractive and full of luxury yachts and cargo/passenger boats. Susie and Ginny spent hours wandering around the shops while I sampled some of the local beer at a waterfront bar. Ibiza Town is serviced by a good local bus service from many resorts, villages and towns around the island which we have used on many occasions. The bus station is located in the business quarter of the town and it is only a short stroll down to the waterfront or old town. We used the local bus from Portinatx on several occasions to go into town and found the short stroll from the bus station was full of interesting sights and sounds. Having been out and about it is now time, in the next chapter, for us to explore the Island in more detail…

Exploring Ibiza

Playa d'en Bossa:

Playa d'en Bossa is, some would say, the most popular resort on Ibiza. Home to famous clubs like Space and Ushuaia and boasting the longest beach on the island dotted with cool beach bars. Playa d'en Bossa offers the visitor everything from budget to 5-star luxury accommodation.

By day the focus is on the longest beach on the island; endless sand and chill-out space with sun beds and parasols. There are cool beach bars with Bali beach beds, excellent food, great service and laid-back music from DJs, it's a summer dream. There is also excellent water-sports facilities. By night, Playa d'en Bossa becomes the focus of the island's clubbing crowd with the island's most popular venues attracting A-list DJs every night. Playa d'en Bossa has loads of cool bars to enjoy a pre-club cocktail; you can even dance on the sand…

Exploring Ibiza: Playa d'en Bossa

Everyday the Spanish flag is seen flying high over the resort of Playa d'en Bossa. Playa d'en Bossa has an excellent choice of accommodation, either right on the beach or just a short walk away. Playa d'en Bossa is one of the most popular resorts on Ibiza, designed for the 21st Century tourist. Recently it has been moving upmarket but not at the expense of those on a budget. In the evening it is time to experience the best, as celebrities and holiday-makers enjoy the vibe of this internationally renowned resort. By day the focus is on the longest beach on the island; endless chill out space with sun beds and parasols…

Exploring Ibiza: Playa d'en Bossa

The relatively new introduction of lounge bars with their Bali beach beds (featured above) and sumptuous healthy menus are blissful, whether you're relaxing after the night before or simply want to be able to reach out and inhale luxury. This obviously comes at a cost but many think that this is well worth the outlay for the weary holiday maker. Add to that great service and laid-back music from DJ's, it's a summer dream for some and an experience to perhaps try just the once for others. For the more active types and if chilling out isn't your thing, the range of entertainment and water sports is sure to grab your attention. When you are planing your next holiday abroad and want to learn how to dive? Then look no further than Playa d'en Bossa…

Exploring Ibiza: Playa d'en Bossa

There are also plenty of shopping opportunities in this resort so if you get tired of the noise, beach, sand and sea you can always do a bit of retail therapy. Once you have spent out or think that it is about time that you got a bit more active and if you like to keep your head above water, it's a spectacular place to try out windsurfing, kite surfing or hire yourself a jet ski. There's also everything in between, think catamaran hire, think having a laugh with friends on a pedalo. Susie and I have not been to this resort but it looks and sounds like it could be on our things to do, places to see list on any future stay on the island. This resort is designed to meet your every whim, with golden sands and beautiful waters. Away from the beach there is an extensive area for shopping. Find yourself the latest beachwear before relaxing with a cool drink and some lunch…

Exploring Ibiza: Playa d'en Bossa

In Playa d'en Bossa there are eateries to suit all budgets and desires. Playa d'en Bossa offers everything from a traditional Irish pub to the celebrity attracting lounge bars, chic, chilled but definitely fun. Such places as 'Outrageous' to 'laid back' can all be found within the shortest of strolls from your accommodation on gloriously warm nights. Only ten minutes transfer from the airport and from Ibiza Town, Playa d'en Bossa is quite rightly one of the top summer resorts both on Ibiza and in Europe. Playa d'en Bossa is fast becoming the place to stay on Ibiza, with a fantastic choice of hotels so why not join the many repeat visitors and make this resort your destination for your next holiday…

Exploring Ibiza: Figueretas

Figueretas is a small suburb of Ibiza Town, with an international mixture of tourists and locals. It has a selection of cafés, bars and restaurants throughout the area, catering for all tastes. Figueretas is a popular resort for all the right reasons. Think palm tree lined promenade, with a golden sand beach and wonderful panoramic views of the Mediterranean stretching before you. Figueretas, a resort that is so good even the locals like to come down and spend time here. Just a short fifteen minute stroll from Ibiza Town in one direction and the famed Playa d'en Bossa in the other direction, it's ideally situated…

Exploring Ibiza: Figueretas

Figueretas, as we have already seen is so near to Ibiza Town and Playa d'en Bossa and offers those staying there the advantage of being near town but still having its own character and style. Figueretas is therefore, a much loved holiday destination for people of all ages. It has a central beach, divided into smaller sections that are in front of the apartments and hotels, and is bordered by a long, palm-fringed promenade. Little ferries depart from the jetties on both ends, to Ibiza town, Playa d'en Bossa and for great daytime excursions to the famous hippy market in Es Caná. You can also get a small ferry to the Caribbean like beaches of the sister island of Formentera…

Exploring Ibiza: Figueretas

In the evening when the sun cools a little but the sea still sparkles, the promenade is lined with artists and craft stalls, lending a distinctly Bohemian atmosphere to the area. The vibe by day is laid back and Figueretas ensures that holds true, with everything from great restaurants on your doorstep and wide vehicle free walkways. This really is an excellent choice for people who want a traditional beach holiday with shopping and good food close at hand and within easy striking distance of a vibrant town centre and harbour close by. Craft stalls, gift shops, restaurants, supermarkets and of course a considerable selection of bars ensures you don't have to leave Figueretas at all if all you really want is to live the "laid back" vibe to the max…

Exploring Ibiza: Talamanca

The picturesque bay of Talamanca is just a short 15 minutes' walk along the marina from Ibiza Town. This is a peaceful resort with a beautiful sandy beach and is ideal for families looking for a beach holiday with easy access to the sites and sounds of a busy town close by. The beach of Talamanca is long and wide, the sand gorgeously white and soft. Although locally known as the 'beach of Ibiza Town' the beach is so big that even in high season it's easy to find your own space. More peaceful than most resorts with no towering hotel buildings in sight, the beach also sports shallow turquoise coloured clear seawaters, perfect for a swim. This really is the location for relaxing in the sun and perhaps enjoying that book you've been meaning to read for years…

Exploring Ibiza: Talamanca

Talamanca is one of the few locations that is open all year round and there are ample bars and restaurants to suit all budgets, serving good food and exquisite cocktails to quench appetites and thirsts. Talamanca is the place to go and let the stress go, far from the madding crowds and even 'out-of-season' this holds true…

Exploring Ibiza: Talamanca

Talamanca's success as a resort is in attracting people who want to go clubbing by night and relax by day. Ibiza Town is just a stroll away, offering some of the best nightlife and restaurants in Europe. Jesus, a small neighbouring village, is also just a fifteen minute walk away and here again, there's a good range of bars and restaurants to tickle the senses. Nightlife exists in Talamanca but it won't wreck your sleep so the beach lovers and family groups get plenty of rest at night ready for another hard day on the beach. Get up early enough and you'll see those clever clubbers walking back to Talamanca across the golden sands at sunrise having enjoyed a night out in Ibiza Town before returning to Talamanca to recuperate peacefully…

Exploring Ibiza: Talamanca

Getting around the island from Talamanca is easy. You can stroll along the promenade for the entire length of the bay, right into the visually spectacular Marina. If you want to go further afield jump onto one of the small ferries and explore the coast in both directions, hopping off at Santa Eulalia or into the Old Port of Ibiza Town, the walls of Dalt Vila are right before you…

Exploring Ibiza: San Antonio

San Antonio, Ibiza, really does offer something for everybody, with a great variety of accommodation and entertainment, and is just a short drive away from Ibiza Town. Susie and I have stayed in this resort in the past and really enjoyed ourselves. Famous for its sunsets and lively night-time vibe, San Antonio is a great holiday choice…

Exploring Ibiza: San Antonio

Susie and Alan on holiday

The resort of San Antonio in the months of May and June, and the later months of September and October are the best times for couples to enjoy the new promenade, the safe, shallow waters of the bay and the fantastic beaches, just a short ferry ride away. The high season months of July, August and the beginning of September are the best time to come if you are looking for buzzing nightlife, when the predominantly British holiday makers are joined by an increasing number of German, Italian, Scandinavian and Dutch guests all ready to party…

Exploring Ibiza: San Antonio

San Antonio is one of the most popular and well-known resorts in the Mediterranean. It is only 20 minutes from Ibiza Town and the airport, has great transport connections to the rest of the island and offers an incredible diversity of entertainment for all ages. The resort is dominated by the beautiful palm-lined promenade which skirts the harbour, constantly busy with yachts, speedboats and ferryboats. This harbour, called Portus Magnus by the Romans, is one of the most beautiful and famous natural harbours in Europe. When we were staying there a USA navy war ship came into port and it was a fantastic sight to see…

Exploring Ibiza: San Antonio

San Antonio beach is a beautiful wide and sandy beach with its safe shallow seawater. It was created in the summer of 2002. There are excellent water sports further along towards the bay. It can be crowded in the high season, so why not catch one of the regular ferries to the nearby beaches on the islands West coast…

Exploring Ibiza: San Antonio

San Antonio today is most famous for its Sunsets and rightly so. Throughout the summer, holiday makers and locals alike flock to the 'Sunset Strip' (just West of the town) to admire the spectacular sunsets over a cocktail or two at one of the many cafés and bars. The 'Sunset Strip' is actually an area called Calo d'es Moro, and is a 10 minute walk from the centre of town…

Exploring Ibiza: San Antonio

All around San Antonio there are magnificent views overlooking the Bay. The main Square with it exotic flowering trees, children's play park and cascading, musical fountains, is the focal point of the resort. It is also the best vantage point for the fabulous annual Fireworks Display which celebrates the fiesta of Saint Bartholomew on the 24th August…

Exploring Ibiza: San Antonio

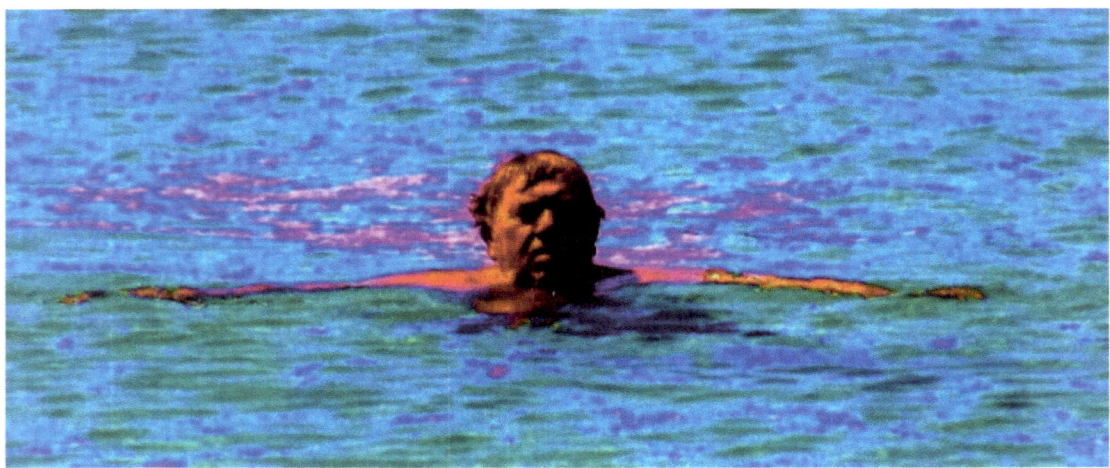

There are many cafes and bars lining the central Square, their parasols adding a festive touch to the holiday scene, and further along the port opposite the yacht club there are some very good restaurants in San Antonio. During our stay in this resort we went to a different restaurant every night for two weeks and did not scratch the surface as far as places to eat are concerned. Susie and I swam in the sea every day and relaxed on the beaches that are all around this resort and when you got tired of one place you just move on down the bay to the next one for a different experience. There is really no need to leave this area as there is everything here that you could want but a trip into Ibiza Town, the county side and to other beaches is strongly recommended. At the heart of the village stands a fine 14th century church. This central area also has a concentration of bars, discos, shops and eateries. Much of the town centre is now pedestrianised…

Exploring Ibiza: Santa Eulalia

Santa Eulalia, is a beautiful town and resort on the East coast of the island. It is popular with families and those looking for a quieter holiday. Santa Eulalia, Ibiza's third largest resort is only 21 km from the airport and many holiday makers return to this resort time and time again for their summer holidays. There is a beautiful, palm-lined promenade running the length of the broad and sandy beach, (which is perfectly safe for the children), and there are some excellent hotels and apartments in and around the town itself…

Exploring Ibiza: Santa Eulalia

Santa Eulalia has a long-established reputation as the island's gastronomic and cultural centre. Shopping in this resort is a great experience for young and old alike, with it's smart shops and pedestrian walkways. You will find upmarket art galleries, lovely sea views, the beautiful and exclusive yacht marina and some of the island's best restaurants. There are also some very exclusive shopping, and a thriving all-year community, ensure that life in Santa Eulalia is led at a rather slower and more relaxing pace. This really is the place if you are looking for a beach holiday that provides a relaxed atmosphere and a safe environment for young children to play all day long. When you tire of the beach a short stroll will take you to some excellent bars and restaurants with the added bonus that the nightlife is more laid back than many of the other resorts on the island…

Exploring Ibiza: Santa Eulalia

Alan waving…

In Santa Eulalia the local authorities and business community have worked very hard together and invested lavishly to maintain its attractions to a more selective visitor and it is now much sought after by those desiring a quieter holiday. A good example of this investment is the seafront promenade, which spans the length of the wide, curved beach, adorned with palm trees, miniature gardens and a large fountain. This is a great place to promenade in the evenings before choosing an eating place in which to spend your evening enjoying a lovely meal and some good local wine. If you want to wander a bit further along the promenade start by facing the sea and then walk along to the extreme right, till you can go no further where you will arrive at the place where the only river in the Balearics runs out into the sea…

Exploring Ibiza: Santa Eulalia

When you have made your way down to the place where the river meets the sea a pretty, peaceful river-walk meanders up to the Roman Bridge which has now been carefully restored. Midway, a footbridge spanning the river gives onto another pretty paved walkway leading to the little beach of Calo de S'Alga in the neighbourhood of Siesta with its small-village atmosphere. In Santa Eulalia there' is a wide range of hotel accommodation, from 5 star hotels to boutique hotels and family-friendly Apartments…

Exploring Ibiza: Santa Eulalia

In Santa Eulalia there are two main streets in which you're bound to see everyone who's anyone at some time or another. The tree lined Calle San Jaime is the main street. It's the daytime meeting place for the coffee and conversation cliques who meet at the tables of the cafes and restaurants to watch the world go by...

Exploring Ibiza: Santa Eulalia

In town and backing on to San Jaime is Calle San Vicente, famous as the Street of Restaurants. Closed to traffic in the early evening, it is transformed into the living, breathing picture of an ideal Mediterranean scene. You will see chairs and tables, laughing promenades and diners, light, music and strolling musicians appear, giving this picturesque street an intoxicating fiesta atmosphere. You can be sure that every night will be a special night out in this resort…

Exploring Ibiza: Santa Eulalia

In the centre of the town a little lane leads from the town hall to the sea, bright with flowering oleanders and hibiscus, colourful with the crafts of street vendors and exhibits of instant portrait painters, ending in the Promenade, the fine white sandy beach and the blue Mediterranean sea beyond…

Exploring Ibiza: Santa Eulalia

When you are in Santa Eulalia and walking along the promenade, you will pass a colourful array of restaurants and cafés, from the cheap 'n cheerful to international exclusive and to the left at the end of the promontory the ferries ply for passengers to nearby beaches, the hippy market in Es Caná, Ibiza Town and for bracing day trips to Ibiza's sister island of Formentera…

Exploring Ibiza: Santa Eulalia:

The impressive yacht marina, has helped make Santa Eulalia one of the focal points of the Mediterranean sailing set. This stylish area has become a favourite for dining, shopping, entertainment and as a place to enjoy the laid back nightlife of the resort…

Exploring Ibiza: Santa Eulalia

Santa Eulalia is the hub of a fascinating colony of very talented people, many of them are world famous. Local galleries and shops have the privilege of selling works by artists who have exhibit in the world's capitals…

Exploring Ibiza: Santa Eulalia

The western approach to Santa Eulalia is across a narrow bridge, with a lovely little Roman bridge to your right. The fascinating 16th century architecture of the Church of our Lady of Jesús, at the summit of the Puig de Missa (Hill of Mass), is beautifully lit at night. From this hilltop you get fantastic views over the municipality of Santa Eulalia which includes Santa Gertrudis, the greater part of Jesús, Es Caná, San Carlos and the beautiful bay of Cala Llonga…

Exploring Ibiza: Santa Eulalia

When leaving Santa Eulalia to the Northeast, the road divides to San Carlos and Es Caná, which are home to the largest and most famous hippy markets on the island. Across the narrow bridge and first left is the pretty route to Ibiza Town, passing Siesta, Cala Llonga, the Ibiza Golf Club and the village of Jesús, all of which are well signposted and are all worth a visit…

Exploring Ibiza: San Antonio Bay

The Bay of San Antonio is famed for being one of the most beautiful holiday locations in the Mediterranean. It has a relaxed friendly atmosphere. Susie and I have had one of our summer holidays to the island here. Along with the thriving resort of San Antonio on the north side of the bay (already mentioned earlier in this book) San Antonio Bay holiday area extends along the south side of the bay. Both locations enjoy panoramic views out to sea and have the most amazing sunsets to be seen anywhere all the year round. In terms of holiday appeal they are two distinctly different resorts hence why this has its own section in this chapter…

Exploring Ibiza: San Antonio Bay

Alan in the sea…

We stayed in the Bay area for one of our summer holidays to the island in the past and found it to have a relaxed friendly atmosphere, perfect for strolling around. By day, you are never far from a beach and at night there's plenty to do and see. On the spacious terraces of the cafes and bars, many have live shows and music until midnight when everyone continues the party inside in air-conditioned comfort or move on to the famous big clubs in town. Or if you have children, like we did, then it is back to the apartment for some sleep before another hectic day on the beach and in the sea begins again…

Exploring Ibiza: San Antonio Bay

In the Bay you are never far from the beach, five small ones and the main beach of San Antonio are within short walking distance and in fact a favourite way to start or end, the day, is a stroll along the shoreline path connecting the beaches that all have bars that open until late all the way along…

Exploring Ibiza: San Antonio Bay

San Antonio Bay has many hotels and apartments to choose from to suit all tastes; most have sea views and are close to the shore line. Many of the island's most beautiful beaches are also on this side of the Island, Cala Bossa, Cala Conta and Cala Tarida are just a short drive, bus or ferry ride away. There's also a good bus service into San Antonio including the Disco bus to the big clubs. We spent most of our days on the beach but did venture to the other beaches mentioned above and into town on the local buses several times during our two week stay…

Exploring Ibiza: San Antonio Bay

In the Bay area gourmet restaurants in the true sense of the word are limited but there are many good restaurants and snack bars with nice interiors and covered terraces along the Bay, many are cheap 'n cheerful but usually you'll receive good, or better, value for money than in town. We visited many such places during our stay and the food was always very good…

Exploring Ibiza: San Antonio Bay

Sunsets are seen almost as well from anywhere around San Antonio and the Bay area. You can take your pick from the numerous beach bars along the Bay or just sit on the beach and enjoy! We always found the time to spend a little time watching the sunset every night of our holiday in this resort. The Bay is justifiably proud that it can more than hold its own when it comes to a variety of live entertainment scenes. Venues range from all types of bars with live or DJ music and others with fun and games. There is definitely something for everyone at good value prices in San Antonio Bay…

Exploring Ibiza: San Antonio Bay

We found that the Bay had its own special feel-good atmosphere. People of all ages and nationalities come here to relax, have fun, enjoy the beaches and sunshine, meet people and to revel in simply being-away-from-it-all…

Exploring Ibiza: Cala Tarida

Cala Tarida has a beautiful, sandy bay on the West coast of the island with a few hotels, apartments and shops. It is very peaceful and family friendly, offering great sun bathing and water sports opportunities. This tiny resort is nestled in a sandy, sheltered bay on the west coast of the island, surrounded by pine-covered hills. It boasts a long beach of fine, white sand (which is south-facing and therefore blessed by sunshine from morning until evening), beautiful clear turquoise and azure seawater, and some of the most amazing sunsets on the island…

Exploring Ibiza: Cala Tarida

Cala Tarida is situated close to San Antonio, which is a fifteen minute bus ride away, or you may prefer to take one of the frequent ferry boats. From San Antonio, there is a regular bus service to the rest of the island. The capital, Ibiza Town, is a thirty-five minute drive away…

Exploring Ibiza: Cala Tarida

In comparison to some of the livelier resorts, Cala Tarida offers a peaceful, tranquil alternative. There are no nightclubs here, but there are some bars and good places to eat so it is ideal for a family beach holiday…

Exploring Ibiza: Cala Tarida

In Cala Tarida there is a supermarket and a few shops and the resort offers great bathing in safe, shallow seawater with water sports also available. Most hotel's in Cala Tarida are high quality hotel complexes close to the beach, providing a wide range of entertainment, sports and amenity, but there are also apartment complexes and private villas catering to a wide range of tastes and budgets. So there is something here for everyone…

Exploring Ibiza: Cala Tarida

On the beach at Cala Tarida the clean, clear seawater over a sandy bottom is shallow to quite a way out on the right, deeper and rocky to the left as you look out to sea. The colours of the sea here are truly magnificent; turquoise, azure blue and emerald green. All this makes Cala Tarida a popular family beach holiday location…

Exploring Ibiza: Cala Tarida

In Cala Tarida there are shops right on to the beach to buy inflatable's, snorkel gear and beach balls. If sun baking just doesn't cut it for you and you have children to amuse then take your bucket and spade along. If you're looking for a solitary spot there's a selection of interestingly shaped rocks to swim out to only just of the seashore…

Exploring Ibiza: Cala Vadella

This is a beautiful and protected bay on the West coast that has a few hotels and apartments and a small compliment of shops and restaurants. Peaceful and family friendly, Cala Vadella offers safe bathing and water sports. Cala Vadella is a beautiful little resort spread over a hillside on the West coast of Ibiza, further along from San Antonio. It's very popular with families in the low and high season, due to the extremely sheltered nature of the bay, the wide sandy beach and shallow seawater and the overall peacefulness of the resort. The main road running through the village is extremely curvy as it winds its way up the hill this means low traffic speeds and a safer environment for children…

Exploring Ibiza: Cala Vadella

In Cala Vadella there is an excellent selection of restaurants and cafes all lining the beach and there can be a lively night-scene in some of the bars. The sunsets are particularly beautiful at Cala Vadella and it is only a 25 minute drive from San Antonio or Ibiza Town. There are good bus connections during the summer months and a shared taxi can also be a good option…

Exploring Ibiza: Es Caná

Es Caná is a small and friendly resort with a good choice of bars and restaurants. It has a crescent-shaped sandy beach, a small harbour for fishing boats, and is home to the famous weekly Hippy Market. Situated on the east coast of the island, Es Caná has all you could want for a relaxing and at times lively holiday. The beach, a pine-fringed crescent of golden sand, is the place to go to chill with a cool drink from one of the bars along its edge or take a dip in the clear blue Mediterranean Sea…

Exploring Ibiza: Es Caná

Surrounding the resort of Es Caná are beautiful unspoiled beaches, easily reached on foot, and the clear seawater, around the resort, offer divers a wonderful underwater world. You will find plenty of friendly hotels and apartments in Es Caná, all very reasonably priced and well located, as well as a great choice of bars and restaurants, from lively pubs to fashionable chill-out lounge bars. Relax by day on the lovely beach, swim in the clear blue sea and by night enjoy a meal in one of the many good quality eateries…

Exploring Ibiza: Es Caná

Es Caná may be smaller than many but is livelier than most so if you want a low key holiday than perhaps it is not for you but for those who seek excitement this resort is ideal. Es Caná is a popular resort on Ibiza's east coast, just minutes north of Santa Eulalia boasting a great central beach, fringed with palm trees, crystal clear seawater and soft sands, watched over by lifeguards and offering more water-sports than you can shake a stick at, Es Caná is fun, fun, fun all the way…

Exploring Ibiza: Es Caná

Es Caná has even more to offer the holidaymaker as just a ten minute stroll to the left of the main beach brings you to Cala Nova beach which is lovely and un-spoilt, this is one of the surfer's beaches on the island, with some cool beach bars serving really good food…

Exploring Ibiza: Es Caná

If you decide instead to stroll just ten minutes in the other direction from Es Caná you will find yourself at Cala Martina beach. This beach is home to the wind and kite surfers of the island. Here you can undertake lessons as well as benefit from the well-respected diving school if underwater adventure is what you seek…

Exploring Ibiza: Es Caná

In Es Caná a tourist train leaves directly from the resort and offers an excellent three hour scenic tour including the historical village of San Carlos, a fully restored 17th century farmhouse and a pit-stop at the visually arresting Cesar's beach bar, before wending its way back to Es Caná. It is a fabulous way to see and understand some of the peculiarities and uniqueness of the island of Ibiza…

Exploring Ibiza: Es Caná

Es Caná boasts a comprehensive range of shopping options and on the outskirts of the resort you will find the amazing and the original island hippy market, so popular that holidaymaker's from other resorts jump on the local ferry services and buses to come and check it out. This is a "not to miss" event. Jewellery deserves a mention here as it's a speciality, inexpensive but beautiful, crafted with silver from India. You will also find great clothing, shoes and handmade leather goods, not to mention a range of art. We enjoyed shopping there very much…

Exploring Ibiza: Es Caná

Es Caná has a little harbour that has stunning views that can be best enjoyed from a range of beach bars, all offering cocktails and food to make sure that every hunger and thirst is firmly quenched…

Exploring Ibiza: Es Caná

Es Caná is well connected to the rest of the island, by bus and also by ferry. Santa Eulalia, Ibiza's third largest town, is just minutes away for fine dining. The surrounding countryside of Es Caná is also very beautiful and worth your admiration. Largely un-spoilt with deep red earth, fields and pine forests the landscape is well worth exploring, also the nearby white-washed village of San Carlos, that was the original hang out of the hippies back in the day (1960's)…

Exploring Ibiza: Cala Llonga

Susie on the beach at Cala Llonga…

Cala Llonga is a complete mini resort with a magnificent wide sandy beach that borders the immensely picturesque Bay with pine clad hills on either side and is one that we have visited during our stays in Portinatx on the island. Ibiza has everything and does everything really well, if you know where to look. This includes looking after families and children and Cala Llonga is the resort that does that best. Everything from the beach activities, accommodation and restaurants are geared up to make sure families have a fabulous holiday…

Exploring Ibiza: Cala Llonga

Susie shopping in Cala Llonga…

Cala Llonga is close to Ibiza Town (excellent shopping and fine dining, not to mention the grand Old Town of Dalt Vila) and Santa Eulalia with its elegant yacht harbour (both just 10 minutes either way), it's a fantastic location for couples…

Exploring Ibiza: Cala Llonga

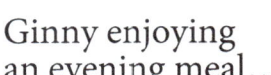

Ginny enjoying an evening meal…

The sea is gently sloping and the gorgeous beach of Cala Llonga, one of Ibiza's biggest, is a huge arc of golden sands, stretching across 200 metres and some 100 metres wide. This allows plenty of space for everyone. There is a children's activities area, including a playground and a mini-amusement park. There are lots of good cafes and snack bars for when you get thirsty and/or hungry…

Exploring Ibiza: Cala Llonga

Although there are not as many shops in Cala Llonga as there are in other resorts, there is still everything you could need, including a pharmacy, supermarket and shops offering everything you could possibly want including some great gift shops for presents to take back home…

Exploring Ibiza: Cala Llonga

Susie and Ginny on the tourist train waiting to go out for the day…

In Cala Llonga parents and couples have not been overlooked and if teasing your toes in the sand as you relax isn't quite enough to keep you occupied there's parasailing, scuba-diving school, windsurfing and water-skiing available. If you fancy staying dry, try your hand at beach volleyball which is a favourite pastime for many on the golden sands…

Exploring Ibiza: Cala Llonga

The resort accommodation reflects Cala Llonga family friendly mentality and there are a host of apartments and hotels in the area, most of them just a couple of steps from the beach itself. At night most of the entertainment is in the local bars and hotels, with a strong emphasis on some really entertaining live acts to keep you occupied and happy on your holiday…

Exploring Ibiza: Cala Llonga

Next to Cala Llonga is the small beach of Sol d'en Serra one of the islands best kept secrets where, if you are lucky, you can watch the full moon rise over the sea as you enjoy your dinner…

Exploring Ibiza: Cala Llonga

If you want to explore further afield by day, one of the most entertaining and relaxing means of transport are the local 'ferries', small boats that inexpensively transport you to Ibiza Town, Santa Eulalia and the renowned Hippie Market in Es Caná which is well worth a day out…

Exploring Ibiza: Cala Llonga

The popular mini resort of Cala Llonga is reached via winding roads with spectacular views. We took a tourist train from our resort of Portinatx that wound it's way through the winding roads and the scenery was truly wonderful. The train then arrived at Cala Llonga and we went onto the wide and sandy beach that borders the immensely picturesque bay with tall, pine-clad hills on either side that ensure this resort is sheltered to form a powerful suntrap, making it popular with those looking for maximum bronzing factor!...

Exploring Ibiza: Cala Llonga

Susie on Cala Llonga beach…

Cala Llonga has shallow seawater that go quite a way out making it safe for children, plus there's the playground area right in the sand. Though many take advantage of the umbrellas and sun-loungers on offer, the large sandy area means there is still plenty of room to chuck a towel down on the sand. So get your flip-flops, sun cream, hat and sunglasses and get down to the beach…

Exploring Ibiza: Cala Llonga

In Cala Llonga snack bars, shops and restaurants are at either end of the beach and dotted along the road. All are within easy reach making sure you want for nothing! The beach itself is lined with busy little cafés and restaurants with a good variety of cuisine. In the resort there are plenty of UK, Dutch, German and Spanish visitors and this is reflected in the range of food on the menus…

Exploring Ibiza: Portinatx

The view of the beach from our balcony…

Portinatx is a complete mini resort, offering crystal clear seawater and stunning scenery, with accommodation and facilities to ensure stress free bliss. We have holidayed in this resort on several occasions and have always enjoyed ourselves very much. It has all a couple or family could want. Situated in the North of the island, Portinatx immediately impresses with not one but three great beaches: S'Arenal Gros (which is the largest), S'Arenal Petit (which is more private) and Playa Porto Beach. Each one of them fully kited out with sunbeds and lifeguards to ensure complete peace of mind and body. Each beach is an easy stroll from all the resorts accommodation and are cleaned and brushed daily…

Exploring Ibiza: Portinatx

Susie and Ginny on a boat trip…

Ibiza is very beautiful and Portinatx is one of the best resorts to experience this. The waters are stunningly clear, making it a favourite with snorkelers and scuba-divers. There are also small ferries boats that will leisurely take you down the coast to the port of San Miguel and even onto San Antonio…

Exploring Ibiza: Portinatx

The local landscape is quite spectacular. The area was the setting for the film South Pacific and when you arrive you understand why it was chosen to represent 'paradise'. There are several good walks to be enjoyed by those wanting to burn some energy by day including a breath taking walk up to the highest Lighthouse in the Balearics where the stunning cliff drop straight down into the clear Mediterranean seawater below. Susie, Ginny and I wonder all the way around the hills above the resort and the views really were breathtaking...

Exploring Ibiza: Portinatx

Portinatx again ticks all the right boxes with a surprisingly active nightlife, where music bars and pubs welcome those who want to throw some moves on the dance floor without being surrounded by 5,000 other clubbers. Good quality restaurants are firmly established in the area and if food is your thing, you'll find everything from restaurants specialising in fish dishes (caught that day) to familiar English pub grub…

Exploring Ibiza: Portinatx

Susie and Ginny by the sea in Portinatx…

In Portinatx the accommodation is plentiful and like the resort as a whole, child friendly. There is even a water park attached to one of the hotels, free for guests staying there and a small charge for those visiting from other accommodation nearby…

Exploring Ibiza: Portinatx

Portinatx is one of Ibiza's best known beauty spots, the little resort is a popular stop on the round the island excursion and while we were on the beach we often saw coach loads of tourist arrive but they did not stay to long so the place stayed fairly quite most of the time. The bay offers magnificent panoramic views, crystalline clear sea water that's great for snorkelling, high, rocky shorelines and a seabed of fine, white sand. There are three good, sandy beaches in this area, all safe for children and offering a variety of activities. When we have stayed there in the past there has even been people selling refreshing slices of fresh fruit right on the beach…

Exploring Ibiza: Portinatx

Ginny and Alan on the tourist train in Portinatx…

There are fantastic scenic walks and spectacular photo opportunities around this resort, so it's worth taking the time to explore. As the beaches are located a short walking distance from the resort there's a good choice of shops, bars and restaurants close by all three. A lovely little tourist train runs from the resort centre to explore other nearby resorts and it takes a very scenic route which we enjoyed very much when we went on it during one of our stays in Portinatx…

Exploring Ibiza: Puerto de San Miguel

Puerto de San Miguel has a broad sandy beach protected by the surrounding cliffs. Situated on the north coast of Ibiza, Puerto de San Miguel was once the fishing port of San Miguel village, but is now a popular small holiday resort with families and couples alike…

Exploring Ibiza: Puerto de San Miguel

Puerto de San Miguel is one of the most sheltered beaches on the island, nestled in a cove and surrounded by lush pine-covered cliffs. A good distance away from the hustle and bustle of the major resorts Puerto de San Miguel is the ideal location for those seeking a tranquil and beautiful location…

Exploring Ibiza: Puerto de San Miguel

In Puerto de San Miguel there are some souvenir shops and a supermarket, and several bars and restaurants line the beach. There are a number of hotels and apartment complexes lining the beach and built right into the cliffs, some of which were built in the early seventies. So whilst not always the most attractive, the stunning sea views from the accommodation more than make up for this…

Exploring Ibiza: Puerto de San Miguel

Puerto de San Miguel boasts a beautifully sandy beach and clear, shallow seawater. There are lots of water-sports, including water skiing, windsurfing and a diving school and, of course, the usual sun beds and sunshades are available to hire. Visitors should definitely visit the interesting drip stone caves which are just a walk up the road on the right side of the bay; the effort will also be rewarded with fantastic views…

Exploring Ibiza: Puerto de San Miguel

Puerto de San Miguel is well connected with the rest of the island by local buses. It is only a short ride to Ibiza Town, Santa Eulalia and the hippy markets. Ferries go to San Antonio, the resort of Portinatx and also the hippy market in Es Caná, they all are well worth a daytime excursion…

Exploring Ibiza: Puerto de San Miguel

The bay of Puerto de San Miguel, which was once the fishing port of the charming village of San Miguel, 5 km to the south. It has a medium sized, deep, curved natural sandy beach. It is protected by pine covered hills, which are delightful for walks if you don't mind the uphill climb…

Exploring Ibiza: Puerto de San Miguel

Although there are a few hotels and apartments situated around the bay of San Miguel, this little bay does not really qualify as a resort. The two hotels built into the rocks are quite unique on the island. There are some good restaurants and a few bars, but no shops (apart from souvenir and beach-wear). Buses run regularly to the village of San Miguel, 5 km to the south…

Exploring Ibiza: San José

The village of San José sits high in the hills in the centre of the highest hill overlooking Ibiza Town and has some excellent restaurants, a church, a few shops and bars in which to sit and contemplate village life. San José is first and foremost a living and working village. It is not a tourist centre so to see Ibiza as it really is a visit here is highly recommended…

Exploring Ibiza: Jesús

Jesús is located in the suburbs of Ibiza Town and you may be surprised to hear that it has some fabulous qualities that will make you want to hang out there. Down the main street are many delightful cafes, shops and bars which create a buzzing atmosphere and a welcoming hub. Jesús is a vibrant village near Talamanca, a favourite with the locals and visitors alike with a great choice of restaurants and bars…

Exploring Ibiza: Santa Gertrudis

The charming village of Santa Gertrudis lies on the geographical middle point of the island, and is a much-loved meeting place for both locals and adopted locals alike. The village of Santa Gertrudis is Ibiza in microcosm. Steeped in tradition, its main square houses the whitewashed church and a cluster of bars, restaurants and shops, whilst in the rich agricultural landscape all around, live sheep, goats and the island's only dairy cows…

Exploring Ibiza: Santa Gertrudis

Many artists, sculptors and musicians have settled in Santa Gertrudis over the years and their work is everywhere in galleries and most famously in the Bar Costa where penniless artists in the hippy era would swap paintings for food and now hanging art competes with hanging hams for space…

Exploring Ibiza: Santa Gertrudis

Santa Gertrudis has expanded rapidly but carefully over the last few years. Smart modern villas now line the new streets, the village square has had a makeover and is now a pedestrian friendly plaza and new, hip café bars and restaurants have joined the more traditional establishments…

Exploring Ibiza: Santa Gertrudis

Any time of day is just perfect for a visit to the village of Santa Gertrudis. In the village shops there are arts and crafts and there are also some good art galleries selling locally produced artwork. The local shops also have an eclectic mix of clothing and accessories so there is plenty of retail therapy to be had here before and after morning coffee, lunch, afternoon tea and/or dinner…

Exploring Ibiza: San Juan

San Juan really is the last village on Ibiza. Arrive here and the only place left to go is the beach at Cala San Vicente, some kilometres down a steep, twisting road through pine clad hills. It's therefore probably the least affected by conventional tourism and a real get away from it all sort of place…

Exploring Ibiza: San Juan

Hippy Market on Ibiza…

Visitors come to San Juan to step back in time to the days when the island was a quiet Spanish backwater. It is also hippie headquarters for those who have moved to the island to seek an alternative lifestyle embracing spiritual philosophy and a healthier way of life. As usual, the village is lorded over by the 18th century whitewashed church. Unusually the rest of the architecture is not all the traditional cubic, bleached white Ibicenco houses. There's an air almost of Atlantic Spain with stone built houses with sloping roofs on the outskirts of the village…

Exploring Ibiza: San Juan

The main street of San Juan is a joy. Quiet, flower bedecked, wrought iron balconies and ancient wooden doors that lead visitors up the cobbles and steps. Here and there you can smell the scent of garlic, the hiss of coffee machines and the chatter of clients in the bars. There's not a lot going on in San Juan, and that's its main attraction!..

Exploring Ibiza: San Juan

From San Juan take a trip down the steep hillside to Cala San Vicente which is well worth a visit for its fine sandy beach and safe seawater. The cave of Es Culleram, a shrine to the Goddess Tanit dating back 2400 years can be found on the way to the coast. The restaurant Can Gat by the beach is such a popular seafood eatery that local people drive for miles just to eat there…

Exploring Ibiza: San Rafael

The small village of San Rafael can be found on the main road between Ibiza town and San Antonio. Like all Ibiza villages it is dominated by its late 18th Century church with amazing views all the way down to Ibiza Town's harbour, busy with cruise ships and big ferries. If open, also have a look inside the village church, it is really beautiful. The two main features of the village itself are the many good restaurants and the pottery workshops…

Exploring Ibiza: San Carlos

Almond blossom on Ibiza…

San Carlos is a small but very well-known village north of Santa Eulalia and is a meeting place for hippies and is home to a surprisingly rich cultural scene. San Carlos became famous as a hippy village in the 60's and 70's as many of those long-haired peace-lovers settled in the beautiful surroundings of this northern Ibiza village. They often lived in old farmhouses, known as 'fincas', often without electricity or even running water!...

Exploring Ibiza: San Carlos

Today, you will still find the hippies in San Carlos. They are the real hippies. For them, being a 'hippy' is a lifestyle, not just a fashion. Here, many prefer to live without modern comforts, with as little money and work as possible and with a true, communal spirit. Time really has stood still here...

Exploring Ibiza: San Carlos

There is a sense of time standing still in San Carlos. For example, old mailboxes made of wood cover an entire wall in Anita's Bar, because even today, there is no postal delivery service to every house in the stunning San Carlos countryside. So many people still pick up their post at Anita's Bar and take the opportunity for a leisurely chat accompanied by a cool drink of squeezed fresh oranges on ice…

Exploring Ibiza: San Carlos

Today's new hippy generation also congregate in Las Dalias, located about 1 km before San Carlos (coming from Santa Eulalia). It is here you'll find one of the most original hippy markets with its hundreds of brightly coloured stalls and larger than life characters. Every Saturday from 10 am until late in the evening, all year round, the sellers set up their stalls on the ivy-covered terraces and courtyards, whilst during the summer months, you can also visit the market every Monday night…

Exploring Ibiza: San Carlos

Susie

Alan

The pretty village of San Carlos has become host to one of Ibiza's most vibrant live music festivals: Ai Carai which takes place every year in June, very close to the Festival of San Juan and is a particularly great time to visit the village. The local Fiesta of San Carlos is celebrated in the weeks around the Patron's Saint Day on the 4th of November…

Exploring Ibiza: San Miguel

The village of San Miguel is truly the gateway to the less developed, rugged coast of the north of Ibiza. Occupying a commanding position, the village and its fortress church, built between the 14th and 18th centuries, dominate the countryside all the way down to the coast at Puerto de San Miguel, which was once the fishing port of San Miguel and is now a popular small holiday resort…

Exploring Ibiza: San Miguel

The church in San Miguel village acts as a landmark to the thousands of tourists who pass through here on route to the big hotel complexes by the coast. It is however, also the venue for high kicking displays of traditional folk dancing as practised by the local folk lore groups on Thursdays from 6 pm in summer...

Exploring Ibiza: San Miguel

In San Miguel village's main square there is a craft market on a Thursday. Here, only products actually made in Ibiza are for sale, and these range from pottery, fresh produce like honey with the scent and taste of the island, bamboo carvings, water colour paintings and handmade sun catchers…

Exploring Ibiza: San Miguel

The village of San Miguel has its fair share of little bars and restaurants. The cave of Can Marça, a former smugglers' hideaway, is an interesting diversion from the port. It is well sign posted and is on the way to hippie heaven, Benirras beach, famous for its sunset drumming…

Exploring Ibiza: Santa Inés

Santa Inés lies to the north of San Antonio in a very fertile region, far away from the tourism of the big towns. It comprises of a church, a supermarket, a few bars and several surrounding houses but not much else, which only adds to the rural charm here. Santa Inés is a wonderful place to visit in order to discover the real Ibiza of the Ibicencan farmers, far away from the hustle-and-bustle of Ibiza Town and San Antonio…

Exploring Ibiza: Santa Inés

It is worth taking a walk around near the village of Santa Inés, as the surrounding countryside is simply breathtaking, with fields of orange, lemon and almond trees set against the deep, ochre-red of the earth and the many different greens of the pine trees…

Exploring Ibiza: Santa Inés

Time seems to stand still in Santa Inés except during the month of February when the almond trees begin to bloom, and the whole of the islanders gather in the village to admire the spectacle. This is one of the prettiest displays of nature you will ever see, as the whole of the valley is swathed in a covering of silvery-white. Although this mostly occurs during February and lasts about 5 weeks, this does depend on the weather. Not so many years back the almond trees began to flower in December after an exceptionally warm spell. Having explored the Island it is time, in the next chapter, to head into Ibiza Town…

Ibiza Town

Alan enjoying a meal on Ibiza…

Ibiza Town offers the visitor everything from the eye catching Dalt Vila, ancient walled upper town with its cobbled alleyways and romantic restaurants to Ibiza Port where you will find some of the world's biggest super yachts moored for the summer. Here you can reserve a table at a range of restaurants on the water front and take in the views of the blue sea, yachts and beautiful people. It is a definite place to be and you'll find plenty of accommodation available in Ibiza Town…

Ibiza Town:

Ibiza Town is a Mediterranean Mecca for the discerning holiday maker and a must for all Island visitors. Take the best of Barcelona, Paris or Rome, with tree lined plaza's, traditional Spanish architecture, romantic restaurants, chilled cafes, colourful markets and the most eclectic crowds and there's only one place you could be and that is in Ibiza Town!...

Ibiza Town:

Ibiza Town offers the best of all worlds, an exciting, cosmopolitan town with fantastic sea views and gorgeous sandy beaches...

Ibiza Town:

Ibiza Town by night is bigger, brighter and better than you could imagine. It is this, that despite its appeal by day, is perhaps what it is best known for. Everything and everyone is catered for. It is great for young, older people and those party people, there's a venue or several in Town to suit every taste…

Ibiza Town:

Susie resting in a harbour side bar in Ibiza Town

Ibiza doesn't stop as the sun goes down or even at midnight. This town celebrates every moment and that means right through the night! This is no sleepy Mediterranean town riding off the back of a few glory moments but the real deal that London, New York, Berlin and the like can but aspire to…

Ibiza Town:

You must climb the steps to the upper town as Susie and Ginny did when we visited the town. I stayed by the harbour due to having poorly knees! Climbing to the top you are better off on foot, in sensible shoes, exploring the narrow, winding, steep cobbled streets and magnificent views from the breaks in the high ramparts and the vast terraces at each level (Dalt Vila actually means 'High Town'). The dramatic main entrance is up a slope, crossing a drawbridge through the Portal de Ses Taules, flanked by mighty statues in roman stone, entering into an ancient cobbled stone courtyard, giving immediately onto the main square…

Ibiza Town:

The other entrance to the Dalt Vila: Portal Nou (reached from behind the Plaza del Parque) has a more gradual ascent. Take your time as there is so much fascinating detail to see. Traditionally black clad Ibicencos, untouched by time or change, go about their lives in the ancient, Gothic Catalan buildings overhanging the streets…

Ibiza Town:

In the upper town sturdy wooden doors that stand ajar reveal spacious stone courtyards and private chapels. The gift shops and art galleries on the walk up to the cathedral are treasure troves of the unusual and unique works of talented local crafts people. There are many first class restaurants in Dalt Vila "Candlelit dinners in a Medieval castle under the Mediterranean stars". Can you imagine anything more romantic?…

Ibiza Town:

Looking down from the battlements by the Cathedral of Our Lady of the Snows, there are some wonderful panoramic views. Look down onto the red tiled cupolas of the 16th century church of Santo Domingo. From here you can also spot the statue of General Joaquin Vara de Rey, the Ibicenco hero of the Cuban War, standing proudly at the centre of the Main Square which bears his name…

Ibiza Town:

In the archaeological museum there are many collections from the Carthaginian era. The museum *Museo Puig des Molins* set in the Carthaginian burial grounds is to be recommended. Ibiza is home to one of the world's most impressive Roman museum collections, with artifacts on display which have been found exclusively on the island…

Ibiza Town:

In the castle a room which contained an exit to the outside of the old castle in Ibiza Town was discovered in 2002 full of pottery, armaments and other objects used in everyday life on Ibiza from Phoenician times right up to the 13th Century. The room connected 2 towers of the castle during the Arab occupation of the island and would have been used as a way for the population to retreat into the castle in times of attack…

Ibiza Town:

The people of the Island had, as a way of stopping the attackers from following them into the castle a custom of filling the room with earth to block securely the entrance from the outside. It is thought that when the castle was overrun by the invading knights from mainland Spain this room remained buried full of earth and was forgotten about until it was re-discovered just recently. This is the reason why all the objects that have been found within it are in such good condition and are giving the archaeologists an insight into life on Ibiza in early times…

Ibiza Town:

Back down the hill from the upper town and into the harbour you will find the yacht marinas on the other side of the port, Marina Botafoch and Ibiza Nueva, are graced with the floating palaces of Ibiza's jet set regulars, who migrate here faithfully at the start of each summer to keep their rendezvous with the most famous nightlife in the Mediterranean…

Ibiza Town:

Around Ibiza Town harbour there are some excellent restaurants and cafés from which to enjoy the view and the atmosphere. Designer boutiques offer great shopping opportunities. When we visit the town I usually take advantage of an outside table to have a cold drink whilst Susie spends her time wandering around the shops and boutiques. Right next to the marina are some of Ibiza's best hotels…

Ibiza Town:

At the end of Marina Botafoch you just have to walk across a road to be at the beautiful beach of Talamanca. Here you have the best of both worlds with a quiet beach whilst being very near the action of the town. From the beach jetty ferries connect the marina to the centre of Ibiza town…

Ibiza Town:

Whether you stay in Ibiza Town or close by or even somewhere else on the island a trip into town is essential. The shopping is great and the restaurants and bars serve all day and all night. After a hard day wandering around sightseeing and shopping why not after dinner go to one of the many bars for a gin and tonic or even a disco and dance the night away. Having enjoyed all that Ibiza Town has to offer it is now time, in the last chapter, to enjoy Ibiza in Colour…

Ibiza in Colour

Sunset at Cala Vadella on Ibiza…

Ibiza in Colour:

The beautiful island of Ibiza…

Ibiza in Colour:

The beautiful island of Ibiza…

Ibiza in Colour:

The beautiful island of Ibiza…

Ibiza in Colour:

The beautiful island of Ibiza…

Ibiza in Colour:

The beautiful island of Ibiza…

Ibiza in Colour:

The beautiful island of Ibiza…

Ibiza in Colour:

The beautiful island of Ibiza…

Ibiza in Colour:

Flying into the sun

The island of Es Vedra off Ibiza…

Ibiza in Colour:

The beautiful island of Ibiza…

Ibiza in Colour:

The beautiful island of Ibiza…

Ibiza in Colour:

The beautiful island of Ibiza…

Ibiza in Colour:

The beautiful island of Ibiza…

Ibiza in Colour:

The beautiful island of Ibiza…

Ibiza in Colour:

The beautiful island of Ibiza…

Ibiza in Colour:

The beautiful island of Ibiza…

Ibiza in Colour:

The beautiful island of Ibiza…

Ibiza in Colour:

Out into the blue Mediterranean sea

The beautiful island of Ibiza…

Ibiza in Colour:

The beautiful island of Ibiza…

Ibiza in Colour:

Rock and waves off Ibiza

Palm tree and a sea view…

Ibiza in Colour:

The beautiful island of Ibiza…

Ibiza in Colour:

The beautiful island of Ibiza…

Ibiza in Colour:

The beautiful island of Ibiza…

Ibiza in Colour:

The beautiful island of Ibiza…

Ibiza in Colour:

The beautiful island of Ibiza…

Ibiza in Colour:

The beautiful island of Ibiza…

Ibiza in Colour:

The beautiful island of Ibiza…

Ibiza in Colour:

The beautiful island of Ibiza…

Ibiza in Colour:

The beautiful island of Ibiza…

Ibiza in Colour:

The beautiful island of Ibiza…

Ibiza in Colour:

The beautiful island of Ibiza…

Ibiza in Colour:

The beautiful island of Ibiza…

Ibiza in Colour:

The beautiful island of Ibiza…

Ibiza in Colour:

The beautiful island of Ibiza…

Ibiza in Colour:

The beautiful island of Ibiza…

Ibiza in Colour:

The beautiful island of Ibiza…

Ibiza in Colour:

Susie celebrating the fantastic sea view at Portinatx on Ibiza

Sunset over Ibiza…

Ibiza in Colour:

The coast of Ibiza

Lizard on Ibiza…

Ibiza in Colour:

The beautiful island of Ibiza…

Ibiza in Colour:

The beautiful island of Ibiza…

Ibiza in Colour:

The beautiful island of Ibiza…

Ibiza in Colour:

The beautiful island of Ibiza…

Ibiza in Colour:

The beautiful island of Ibiza…

Ibiza in Colour:

The beautiful island of Ibiza…

Ibiza in Colour:

The beautiful island of Ibiza…

Ibiza in Colour:

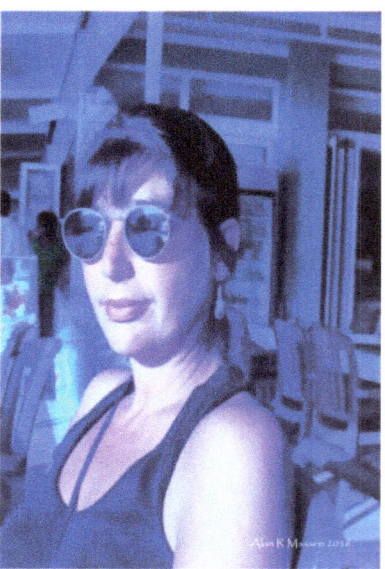

Ginny, Alan, Cat and Susie on one of our holidays to Ibiza…

Ibiza in Colour:

Susie enjoying our holiday on Ibiza…

Ibiza in Colour:

Ginny and Susie enjoying a boat trip on Ibiza

The beautiful island of Ibiza…

Ibiza in Colour:

Susie and Alan enjoying times out in Portinatx…

Ibiza in Colour:

Susie and Ginny playing crazy golf in Portinatx…

Ibiza in Colour:

The beautiful island of Ibiza…

Ibiza in Colour:

Susie out and about on Ibiza

The beautiful island of Ibiza…

Ibiza in Colour:

Ginny and Susie in Portinatx on Ibiza

The beautiful island of Ibiza…

Ibiza in Colour:

Susie relaxing in the sun on Ibiza

Alan and Susie on the beautiful island of Ibiza…

Ibiza in Colour:

The beautiful island of Ibiza…

Ibiza in Colour:

The beautiful island of Ibiza…

Ibiza in Colour:

Ibiza Island of Dreams

As we come to the end of our journey it is time for me to say goodbye. I hope this book will inspire you, when you are planning your next holiday, to consider going to the paradise island of Dreams that is Ibiza - **HAPPY HOLIDAYS**...

Acknowledgement

I would like to acknowledge and thank ALL the people of Ibiza who have helped make all of our holidays to their beautiful island, over the years, such a positive and happy experience for us. Our holidays, in the past, have been centred in Portinax and San Antonio Bay but we have also found the time to visit many of the resorts, villages and Ibiza Town featured in the pages of this book.

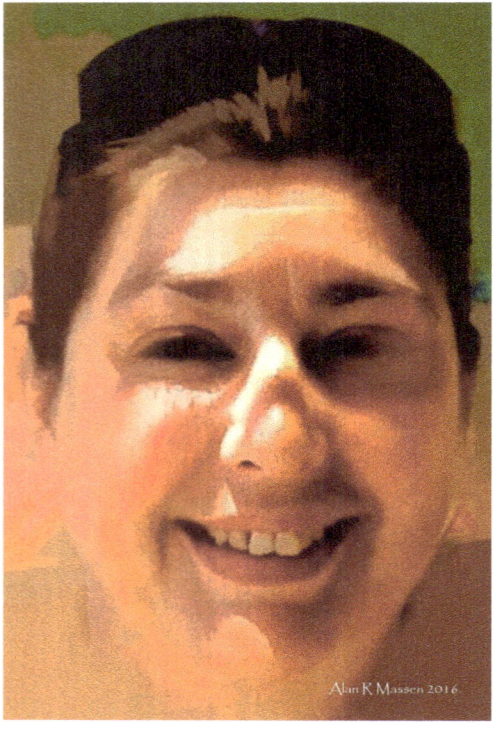

Susie and Alan

Just before I go and finally, for me, the most important thing to help and ensure that you enjoy your holiday to the full is that you have someone special who you can share your holiday experiences with. I am very lucky, I have my wife Susie as my companion on our Mediterranean and UK holidays. Her smile, laughter and enthusiasm has made every day of our stays abroad and at home enjoyable and memorable. So until the next time always remember to smile and be happy.

Copyright © 2019 Alan R. Massen

Thank You

www.ingramcontent.com/pod-product-compliance
Lightning Source LLC
Chambersburg PA
CBHW042227010526
44113CB00045B/2834